# UNION

# UNION

POEMS BY DON SHARE

Zoo Press

Zoo Press • P.O. Box 22990 • Lincoln, Nebraska 68542
Printed in the United States of America

Distributed to the trade by The University of Nebraska Press
Lincoln, Nebraska 68588 • www.nebraskapress.unl.edu

Cover design by Dana Frankfort © 2002

Cover painting, *#1 Psalm Praising* by D. Share, 1994 © Don Share

*Bridge with Moon #1* © J&D Richardson Stock Photography

Additional design work, LeAnn Jensen

Share, Don, 1957-
  Union / by Don Share.— 1st ed.
    p. cm.
  ISBN 0-9708177-7-0 (alk. paper)
  I. Title.
  PS3569.H3423 U55 2002
  811'.54—dc21
                                        2002012453

zoo008

*First Edition*

# Acknowledgements

Grateful acknowledgment is made to the editors of the following magazines, in which these poems appeared, sometimes in slightly different form: *AGNI*: "Saviour" and "Wine"; *Harvard Review*: "Refrains"; *The Journal*: "To the Angels"; *New England Review*: "Spiced"; *The New Republic*: "I have seen, my Celalba..."; *The Paris Review*: "Grit"; *Partisan Review*: "The Story"; *Poetry*: "For Laura"; *Salamander*: "Divorced," "Arch," and some of the poems used to divide the sections; *Salmagundi*: "At Seventeen" and "Semele Speaks to the Wind"; *Witness*: "Dilemma".

"Divorced" also appears in *Outsiders*, edited by Kurt Brown and Laure-Anne Bosselaar, Milkweed Editions, 1999.

Assistance and vital support from the Corporation of Yaddo is most gratefully acknowledged.

This book is dedicated to Jacquelyn Pope,
and Madeleine, with all my love.

# Table of Contents

## III

"Birds live their lives in air"

I

I have seen, my Celalba, strange things:
 split clouds, broken-mouthed winds,
high towers kissing their own foundations,
 and the earth expelling its guts;

bridges bending like tensile stems;
 prodigious streams, violent rivers,
bad crossings through great currents
 and worse bridlings in the mountains;

days like Noah's, fine people
 in the highest-rising pine trees,
in the greatest, most robust beech trees—

shepherds, dogs, cabins, and cattle,
 over the waters I saw them, formless, lifeless,
and nothing more than my own cares troubled me.


 —*after Góngora*

# Signals over Hill

I was one of the babies who boomed,
whose parents left home
and came back, prosperous, on car trips
in Plymouths packed with
Triptiks, Thermoses and kids,
to apartments dense with Readers' Digest
Condensed
Books, condensed milk, the family Bible,
savings passbooks, Nero Wolfe and Mickey Spillane paperbacks,
flatware, stemware, Purex,
boxy clock on the mantel,
vial of rose water,
dresser filled with shirts still in cello,
the Olds 88,
coffee table ash collectors,
and sepia portraits of the vanished.
In this world of fins and aerials I loved
a battered traffic sign that promised,
"Signals Over Hill."
Once we passed over this hill,
our magicmarkered routes traversed,
the peanut gallery would cheer,
*Germantown,*
where those who took us in
were always proud of something,
always handing us dimes,
always clasping our hands
till at last, they gave up their
last gasping, odd-accented ghosts,
knowing that roots
are, themselves, a form of rootlessness.
They lived on Linden Boulevard,

which was not a boulevard,
and had no lindens,
but squat hydrants rooted on side-
walks overwritten with cracks
that inscribed indelible, plotless tales:
People lived, died, quietly as possible,
in postwar solitudes of lightless
living rooms, views into other apartments
like framed photos,
with other people's cooking odors,
and echoing hallway voices.
They told, and retold,
stories that drifted into notions
like butterflies reluctant to alight.
Mornings unveiled the sunlight
and bustle of hope
for the monoglottal young.
Afternoons: a film of familiarity,
the Sabbath wine of absentmindedness.
Sunset registered on magic-eyed Magnavoxes and Zeniths,
till we dozed with Jack Paar,
his adult jokes bewildering me,
and the garden flowers of memory closed
for us all, sleepy together on the Castro Convertible,
each unaccented daisy the day's eye.

# Dilemma

At Shiloh, creek water spills
braided, dignified, full of memory,
like old shape-note music.
There is no sign of the future here,
And the past? All murk.
Dark rain drizzles down slick
as beads of tin-dipper whiskey.
The land seems drunk
on it: ridge, path, and brier.
Everything is wet, unhurried.
The Tennessee River feeds young oaks,
and it is a pleasure to see them.
Nothing sings through their leaves yet,
the bark hasn't crusted, and a pure
high mist halos each one. . .
My fire has died out,
and the road back glisters at the ice-point.
Need sends me through unanealed wilderness
to one of the dole-fullest spots of ground
on the whole earth: Memphis.
Where the past still hurts, and gets sung about.
Where the Mississippi flows by without anguish.
Where I was born.
I'll tell you something.
The past? It is going, or gone.
Yet this isn't the end of it.
We saw a big need, and we filled it.
But not even a war set everybody free.
In the original catastrophe of our history
we became Christ-haunted, contrapuntal.
We fought America in ourselves.
We pitched a dilemma, and it still
heaves us around on its wild horns.

# Wine

Here's to us!
And here's to the gods of destruction!
It's not possible for me to love
anybody who speaks to me as you do.
I've been spoken to
already in that voice,
and I do not intend to be drunk
on it again, so long as I live.
You are the one I adored.
Here is the last glass of wine.
It's a paradox
that whatever lives invites
its opposite.
I can't see why grapes
should sing, and we should argue.
Here is the sea.
It contends with itself, and
with the other.
If you could be gentle,
I could be a man.
I want to learn this evident
form of sunlight, color, and intoxication.
I need to know particulars:
Dregs. Water. Air.
Here are the elements,
on our table, of love,
another sort of wastage.
A good vintage: a year.
I could not know you.
You could not know me.
But what is there under the skin
of love, but love?
The yeast, the fruit, the spice.

And love's ashen bouquet.
What wakens us to daylight?
What makes us live?
I could drink you,
then the dream would come true.
Love someone else, instead.
There is always blood to flow.
And water.
And wine.
I've made a decision,
Heaven knows. It knows everything,
and we are in the dark,
with love-spun hearts, and wine.
I hope the angels will consent
to call us lovers.

# Saviour

What would a Saviour make of our half-thoughts?
He is busy with the skirt of rain,
the bric-a-brac lands birds flee from,
the zoning sun. Before redeeming any more
of the landscape, He would know its true color,
and who sees it. Saviour? Means taste.

*

Surely He would know
we have capitulated
in every way.

*

Even the best blood
pools in beds
under an equator of slaughter.

*

God makes only geniuses,
but our idiom grows crooked, its marrow
a broken skeleton's. Yet
till the air becomes air again,
there is always something that can be learnt,
even in the awful grates of death.

*

*If the salt*
*hath lost its savour*
*wherewith*
*shall it be salted?*

*

Where is the so-called fat of the land?
The thick branches respond
to rain
in jewelled form.
Hence, leaves.
Hence, bees keen on the blossom,
blackbirds drawn from the life.
Round May
the land gorges,
while the crow is always starved.

*

Earth totters,
lifts up its horn to the heavens
while its inhabitants grow yet
rich and poor together
and speak with insolent neck.

# Faithful

Faithful in appearance but errant
in its innards, our house tocks and ticks
like an inherited clock whose hour-hand sticks.
Its moods, softly articulate,
irregular, punctuate the minutes
without object, as if to say,
*Something about us isn't even us.*
The cat is ill. Our fence, unmended, these days
lies chock-a-block in segments
in the yard. A hard winter rime glazes
the soil, carefully composted in the garden, while
our bare young maple, unable
to sustain itself, seems to ache with cold.
The stairsteps creak and strain
to make sense of the season.
Sighs, the eiderdown, a musty waft
from the furnace, the winds that race—
these sap the afternoon, indicate
that life has a length
which is no length, measured
against the sturdy blocks
and slab on which it is founded:
this place will outlive us.
A black crow has rounded
our cul-de-sac in a clock-face
of circular solitude: it will come back.
It will never grow old.

# Self-portrait in the I-Zone™

*(after Ugo Foscolo)*

Forehead, furrowed; my eyes, intense, sunken;
Hair, dusky; cheeks, ashen; expression, ardent;
Lips, thick, slow to laughter, drawn-in;
Neck, fine; head, bent; chest, hairy;
Limbs, set; clothes, simply chosen;
Step, rapid; thought, faster;
Kindly; bristling; open; prodigal; sober;
World-averse, as events go adversely for me.

Sad most days, and alone; forever in thought;
Fear mixed with hope leaves me obsessed;
Modesty makes me vile; anger makes me strident;
My mind articulates warnings, yet my heart,
Full of vices and virtues, rants—
*Death, you owe me fame and rest.*

# For Laura

While we were swimming, a butterfly
dipped past the pool.

Sunshine forced the ripples
to glow like bent halos,

and the black marker lines shivered
like brain waves in their final cogitations.

What were your thoughts as the butterfly
drifted to graze the weeds?

Why did the one and only sea-breeze
tip the treetops with false stars?

I only know that as my hands passed over
and around you, time endstopped,

and that we leaned back from our last kiss
the way one tree bends away from another for light.

The last darkness that closes my eyes,
that leads me away from white day,
will release my soul
from the endless flattery of anxiety;
but my soul won't leave memory behind
on the shore where it burned;
its flame will swim through cold water,
defy the harshest Law;
so my heart, which God made a prison,
my veins, which fed such fire,
my marrow, which burned so gloriously,
will vanish, unlike my desire:
it will be ash, but ash which can feel,
it will be dust, but dust in love.


—*after Quevedo*

# Refrains

So I broke our wedding vows,
Which, I realize,
Have no if's, but's, or and-how's;
But her eyes
Grew hard as quartz:
Her eyes were broken hearts.

I am odd, and getting older.
Maybe the secret of love is to let
It get, like the unscalable peaks, colder.
She was the hottest thing, my tropics, and yet—
Each season passes. But to forget
Her is impossible no matter how long ago
It was she got wind of this, and let me go.

Time is passing boring.
And for all my whoring
And point-scoring, and the scolding, and lurid
                luring of me
She did during her leaving me, I see
That a single vain year has come and gone
Since the time I went back to, as in cradle, lying alone.
I am odd, and getting on.

Certain as rain,
The kind of recurrent pain
A woman receives from the storming man.
What does he do but go on in this vein,
Yelling, surging, inserting and asserting
                wherever he can?

Time rains; it rains.
Still the fever runs along my veins—
I am a donor, a bleeder, a waiter-in-vain, for love's
                    sickled banns.
*When cocks go up, down go the brains,*
So the gypsy proverb goes; born in caravans,
My fathers' blood ran hot and cold; when they suffered,
                    they suffered in refrains.

# Spiced

That day I held my head in my hands,
crouching on the dry soil
of what had been our garden,
and you seemed to tower over me, the way
the sunflower lords itself over mint:
head sternly bent, supple, transient,
while I fell uprooted across flagstones.
Things that we see as ornamental
grow fundamental, like the leaves
and wild blossoms withering on the lawn
at the end of a backbreaking weeding session;
they, like the sunflower, like the massive
blueberry bush or thick thorny rose,
each plucked from the same earth,
would still have soil clumped to their roots
as if everything varied is joined, strangely, underground.
After we separated, I noticed that pulled weeds,
sometimes re-root after a few rains
if left uncollected on the ground,
a kind of resurrection before death.
Sometimes, things escape.
Sometimes, green and spiced,
they rise from the same vivid earth.

# Ending is a True Marriage

Pulling up
Pinocchio's noses,
the seedlings everywhere
among the early roses,
you bite your lip,
pull at your hair.

*Green shoot*
*from brown husk.*
*From dawn's root*
*to withering dusk.*

They have the world to go to.

*

Our separation
brings spaciousness
to my life.

I make time
to stand alone
in the garden;
I notice
the differing sunsets,
listen to the loquacious
evening dogs.

I let mosquitos
have my blood,
and open
my house to ants.

Solitude is a bargain;
I hold up my end.

                *

I bury
banana peels to nourish
new roots of pepper plants.

I leave some
to welcome the slugs,
who thrive on delay,
who leave traces;
who can't be told
one from the other.

                *

The seeds
of weeds
feed butterflies
which scour
the browning lawn
for rest.

I forget my work.

*Either the crop is planted,*
*or it's not;*
*either the crop is weeded,*
*or it's not;*
*either the crop is harvested,*
*or it's not.*

Earth didn't eat
the apple
in Paradise:
a man and a woman did.

I forget my work.

     *

It makes sense
for bees
to nest near
honeysuckle

for black crows
to stalk green grass,
and for blue tips
to form early
on pine trees.

A thrush
steps
out on a limb
to sing.

As he leaves
the branch
it dances,

empty.

This makes sense.

     *

*Green shoot*
*from brown husk.*
*From dawn's root*
*to withering dusk,*

It makes sense.
I make time
to hold up my end.
We have the world to go to.

# Semele Speaks to the Wind

I know there are three Fates:
one spins the thread of a woman's life,
another cuts it off when the time comes,
and what the third does, I forget.
I forget things because of Jupiter.
He had Io in a cloud;
she could not love him as he was—a god.
Even Europa could barely hang on.
But I demanded that he come
to me the way he came
to his own wife on Olympus.
What I got was a thunderbolt
that shortened my life, if not my desire.
Thunderbolt: the blasted line
that divides mortal from god. How odd,
this struggle, this mist of passion and *sfumato,*
this ash junked on the ocean's waters.
Now I know why they call it transport,
why Demosthenes fractured rhetoric
by trying to outshout the waves.
That's the way it is with the tide...
That's the way it is with gods...
That's the way it is!

# Old Highway 78

Driving to Byhalia
on Old Highway 78, I gun my Sunbird
and a cardinal takes off like a shot.
Last night it rained and flooded,
and today there is a freeze; steam
rises ghostly from the Coldwater River.
Oil kicks up from the blacktop.
I veer down a gravelled,
rutted, off-the-map
county road, and skirr
past a blur of Nativity scenes,
one after the other,
that look like improbable cookouts.
This is a belt not of Bibles,
but subsistence farms
with propane tanks,
spray-painted nameboards, and leaning
silos of soybeans.
Down here the dogs
are in charge, and keep their snoots
level as the barrels of shotguns.
Meanwhile, vacant porch rockers
sway idly in the Gulf wind. Arrows
twist like the s's in "Mississippi"
on successive roadsigns
which have been ignored, so the skidmarks
tell, except for target practice.
The afternoon is over,
and I haven't seen a soul.
Yet good hearth-smoke
stealthily fills the iron-colored sky
and mixes with the clouds.
There is just now

the intransigent vapor
of what turns old plow points
to rust,
and even my wistfulness
is mist. But the earth I see
peripherally, as the Sunbird skims a shoulder,
will be turned up again in spring,
and those legible furrows, these cresting roads
will remain familiar,
arch, loop, and whirl,
like handwriting I remember.

# Leaf

Remember our difference
about the rose-of-sharon?
When it refused to extend
a single twig,
and looked as though it would
never prosper, you extracted
it from the special spot
it held in the yard;

Remember our difference
about whether to let mint
run free in the garden?
When it went berserk,
refusing to respect
your stone borders,
you waited
till I went out of town,
and uprooted each pungent sprig.

This work,
pruning our marriage
to the soil
line, was over by fall.

As I think of you,
long gone, remarried,
the house sold,
my eyes still cloud,

and the dry thorn
of my heart, hidden now
from sun, rain, and crow,
in a plot I can't neglect,
excruciates its last faithful leaf.

# The Story

Sick in the craw,
on a prolonged binge,
I wrestled naked-handed with love.
Like the wrack and maw
of weather, this was a seamy
ravishment, taking place *peu à peu.*
You were the woman.
And when you said, "Love is hard
to surrender; it is wrong to give
so much," I knew
it was all up with us.
You know the story:
Shylock and me?
We both had feelings.
We both got cut.
The right wind brings tears,
even to the biggest bastard's eye.
It's the dictatorship
of the visible effect:
Our washing (my white shirt,
your black slip) hangs
stiff in the yard,
while winter branches freeze,
yet still flex and sing.
Like mending thatch,
or rhyming rats to death,
bending and contrition are lost arts,
and songs no longer move maids.
Marriage has its own desolations.
I have plain intentions.
Yours were bold.
The shifting moon knows some
of this woe:

Hers is a history
of exquisite classifications,
ours a story
of divestment
that remains to be told.

# My Luck

Today, just my luck,
a storm washes the air and churns
wind into my face
as I approach once again the roseate
eye of our great, stunning church.

Lord, who works
the infinitesimal seed of April,
why such cruel old rains?

Why the sinewy clouds, full
as time,
why the star-tipped horizon,
the comets
always wrinkling beyond us?

I come here so that my heart,
blown leaf, may rest.
I lurch toward the threshold, and a gust
bows the umbrella's head.
Afternoon's chimes ring.

Where is the hand that grasps
wind? Where
the shape and form of God,
the simplest luck,
the necessary blessing to find a blessing?

As I reach the sanctuary door,
rain beads like a rosary in my hand.

# Rivers

I hug shadows, and they disappear;
in dreams, my soul tires;
alone night and day, I fight
the hobgoblin I hold in my arms.
I try to haul her in,
and seeing my sweat roll away,
I end up more stubborn,
stuck in a love that breaks me.
I want revenge: her false image
refuses to leave my sight;
she mocks me, which makes her happy.
I go after her. I lose my spirit,
yet I reach her, feel that I must run
behind her, and drown her, crying rivers.

# Divorced

The air swimming with the bugs' forlorn Morse code
    on a hellish mid-morning;
Lakewater spitting at us with each choppy oar-splash;
Boys in baseball caps on passing shells who return no greetings;
Arthur Conquest yelling unintelligible insults about my J-stroke;
Jane in the bow shovelling water fiercely in all the wrong
    directions;
Brick factory buildings clogging the banks of the seedy Charles
    from Newton to Waltham;
Culverts, water-lilies, water-bottles, branches, rope,
    and sun-sparkle making me afraid to drown;
An old woman pausing in slow surprise on an overpass as she sees
    us thrashing;
The sun moving with no visible circumference, the sky flat,
    cloudless, high;
The wind insistent, our rhythm inconstant, my thoughts divorced.

III

Birds live their lives in air,
fish in water, salamanders in fire,
and man, who gives everything birth,
is all alone on earth.
I, myself, born for torments,
feel at home in the elements:
my mouth sighs into the air,
my body wanders earth, everywhere,
my eyes fill with water day and night,
while fire sears my soul, my heart.


—*after Quevedo*

# Sweet Life

Our house was for sale,
which was a virtuous herb against melancholy.
When the idea first came to you,
your eyes danced like jam-jars of moonshine
thanks to self-love, that violent prayer.
It's a sweet life, you said,
anyplace we never lived.
Magnolia blossoms dropped,
and when your mood burnished,
the river blushed dark and the Pyramid blinked pale.
Like a backward cousin I steadied
myself, and glanced around for sympathy
among the vacant cobblestones—
we kissed, and this deal, our last, was sealed.
We walked arm in arm through spent Confederate Park,
following the noisy jackdaw, the croaking gull,
and Jupiter's eagle,
until we came upon two dead elms
pulled up, like us, by the roots.
The house finally sold, we left
certain things trapped in old attic trunks there
like the treasure of Egyptian kings
at home in their tomb-cities,
and let our half-burned vows warm the hungry air
along this Nile we call the Mississippi.

# In Order

Nobody knows the blossom so well
as one whose apprenticeship
ends with autumn;
nobody moves so arduously in the sun
to skim nectar at his peril:

*the secret of life is*
*to fail without killing yourself*

and as the honeybee, trapped
behind a windowscreen, angry at the housecat,
falls behind the miniblinds
stinging and losing,

*when I try to look into your opaque eyes*
*I see nothing; it stings*

So summer's last leaves blow
banded in paling sunlight,
and as the weather turns just now
too cool to stay outside,

all our affairs soften
into the collected past,
the honey all gone
from hives closed by winter's reach

*and I reject happiness in order,*
*precisely in order, to remember it.*

# Spiritual

How many times
I had seen my father-in-law, Jim Tatum,
fishing down there,
heard him sing those withering old spirituals.
Once, I asked him
what he was fishing for.
Before the wind drowned him out,
I heard him say,
"Sweet life."

And when he moved on to the Firestone plant,
where he worked like hell after the farm flopped,
they built Libertyland
on the bluff where
we used to watch the Arkansas cottonfields flood,
and started calling Confederate Park something else.
Both he and the city began to sink at last.
Long after the flooding and the sinking,
when the Mississippi forgot where it was headed,
I still heard that singing.

When they closed the plant,
those lean years spent for a mean wage
ended with an obvious joke about the company slogan:
"It's time to retire."
He hid from his family,
drifting on the lake at Tunica
in a small boat full of small bass
with a few leftover hooks, killing off bourbon in a shot,
till his heart gave out for the first time, and he fell right in.
Cousins fished him out,
and his picture got in all the papers.

After that, he slept in a darkened room all day.
The Chevy went unstarted for months,
the lawn grew brown, and Grandma was struck old
as if by June lightning.
Their cross-prescribed medicines lay uncapped on the dresser,
the shotgun rested faithful in iron rust by the door.

He ended up a tired man who woke up half-cocked
and lonely, panting in a halo of cigarette smoke,
reeling off stale stories over old coffee—
grim tender memories, significant, deeply
fueled by real love and cheap marine gas.
The family reunions in Yazoo City over forever,
I last saw him swimming
in floral arrangements from the Catholic neighbors
at the chapel by the river
on the first spring afternoon when you could smell the magnolias.
His last words were, "God made us one hell of a river..."
Say whatever you want,
the man always shook you by the hand
and gave you every drop of wisdom he ever had.

*"God made us one Hell of a river."*

# Stones

A stone will never look you in the eye.
A stone takes on appearances, if instructed.
A stone says whatever it is told to say.
A stone may well lie mute for a millennium.
A stone is all weight and brawn, without spirit.
When a stone flies, it is only when launched
        by the violent hand of man or nature.
Even stones crumble; you find them around ruins.
A stone means division.
Jails are made of stone.
A tiny stone will injure the foot of a man who has
        walked many miles.
A stone left at a gravesite is a sign of misery.
The poor can not eat stones.
A stone unpaired releases no spark.
The stone has no grasp.
At the bottom of fathomless waters:
        stone.

# Prayer

Someone plays music.
Someone breaks his fiddle

On a stone.
Two brothers

Flail, bellies full of Jack.
They sink into cots.

Stunned,
Twelvemonthed,

Stones in the river
Turn heavy.

We turn bitter:
Meaner than death

Adamant, dispossessed,
Fools with battles,

We stay drunk
On doom.

Our eyes
Run with veins

While the stars, as always,
Stare us down.

The foamed Gulf
Flares out at us

Forever.
De-Eastered,

We pray for the dead
In bone-English

And dream long
On the monogram of Christ:

*Lord, simplify us,*
*Remember us.*

# Shady Grove

The heat drove me and Cleo-the-Basset
To the grace and cling of the impartial woods
Back of the clamber and blear of our street.
Like a mini-chain gang, we mauled the grove, winded,
Worked our own private wills, green-shaded.
This was before the nation, off-stage, had the goods
On Nixon, before my ring-finger was bonded gold
In wedlock, before Cleo turned blind-eyed, old.
Twists of branches and root. Dogsmell, and sweat.
The archaic slur of my accent hadn't left me yet.
Cleo and I snuffled Memphis loam like it was Heaven.
1969 was all wisdom teeth and no wisdom for me, then.

# Grit

On a Washington Heights corner in the panting swelter,
I learned that 'grit' was not hominy, or teeth, but proud squalor.
Not deficiency, but irritated worldly brick-chip-poster-tatter.
D.G.'s pugilistic grandpa was late to meet us. It was beginning
       to matter.
I couldn't get the subway squeal out of my ears, was starved for
       a hot dog,
Resolved, that summer, to feast off the whole hog,
Unpenned from metallic cart with mustard-ketchup colored
       umbrella.
Or: deli food, savories like *provolone, mortadella...*
(We had no such in Memphis, where 'Italian' food meant 'fried.')
We were terrified that Mister G. had been mugged, or had died,
Left to ride a sweaty bus route to fatal places
With names like 'Hell's Kitchen,' among unfamiliar faces.
He turned up with a black eye like a bull's eye.
A seatmate had tried to rob him—though all he did was try.
Mister G. boasted, in his misnomered cold-water flat,
As we roasted: *I sure showed him what was what!*
We drank iced-coffee. There was Yiddish on the radio.
I was seventeen, third-rail thin; Mister G., plump, dying,
       and eighty or so.

# At Seventeen

Morningside Heights. Fall, 1974.
A Broadway hardware store.
A clerk wants to sell me a hammer
For 20 dollars, damn her.
Away from home, first sweltering week of school,
I leave, enraged, without the tool,
Hearing myself shout, feeling afloat:
*Hey! I dint just get off the boat!*
My best Apple accent, too,
And for emphasis: *Fuck you!*
The unvarnished truth is,
I was ashamed of having been raised in Memphis.
And for months and months, while I read the Great Books
I suffered higher cabfares, jokes, funny looks
From prep-school boys
Who had no accents, but lots of poise.
Despite the Columbia curriculum,
I turned book-smart, but stayed Manhattan dumb
Till I tore down, plank-by-plank, the lank and haul,
The trill that was not Trilling, the occasional *y'all*
Of a lazy-built, leaky drawl.
Perhaps the trauma
Does not now sound like drama.
It wasn't the stuff of myth, but all design is Procrustean:
Who would do now what he did back then?
This was my first adult choice.
I unboarded the home that was in my voice,
Bullheadedly bulldozed its pennynail past.
It was not worth the cost.

# Dispatches from the McDonald's on Union Avenue

*(to Gen. N.B.F.)*

You built bulwarks of stone on Union,
But the land lies face flat in eternal surrender.
Its capitulation is gold and expensive.

The dead are forever sheltered
From your provocations, and the living,
Helter-skeltered, can't remember.

Even the day half-tarnishes in sinking light
As, like your vanquished neighbors,
You remember everything, but foresee nothing.

\*

In a well-groomed park on Union,
The low boughs are spare as skeletons.
Wind scores the tree-trunks like dice.
You are a statue now, a Confederate in effigy,
Whose bronze horse never flogs its stiff tail.

\*

From war, Sir, there is yet no rest.
Money's in the river, and blood's in the sod.
The blue sky is harassed by one grey cloud.
Your face, like the sun, is set.
The traffic on Union is sadistic and scared.

\*

There would be no bronze here
Were there not also grey in the wind
    and blue flung into the river.
The War? It's over.

History pales and flakes away,
While its memorials withstand every kind of weather.

*

At the McDonald's on Union, Old Glory
Flaps North, a keen nuisance to the senses.
As you knew, great force usually wins,
While a wind never ends.

*

Your grandest enemy, Grant, subdued the city.
He had the newspaper editors put behind bars.
Today, the *Commercial Appeal* has offices on Union.
It has sections called "Real Estate" and "Neighbors."

*

At Baptist Hospital, on Union,
Hurricane season takes the place
Of rage, and death does no little harm, either.
Wars are memories of wars,

Though if we forget them, history does us one better.

*

At the very end of Union, forked
Like Shiloh's wormwood fences,
Roots stake their slow claim,
While rooks gun for the squirrels.

The blue sky at last finds grey clouds its equal.
As for the river, there is always danger
In such waters. The day runs red at sunset,

And the temperature is hot and violent.
Wives go to ground with their husbands,
Their children grown wicked in newly-built homes.

## Pax Americana

July kindles the redneck in me.
I blaze down Interstates
that are viaducts for my beery nerves

and remember what hell these roads
are paved with...
If I don't keep moving,

I could end up divorced, or flat-out broke.
I could end up up-the-creek without a paddle.
I could end up dead and gone and good for nothing.

In the old days,
I was one of the local vandals,
setting fires, tossing cats down perfectly

good well-heads, exploding princely toads.
It was hot and weird,
and Jane and I'd just graduated;

we liked the sound of sirens.
The cops, good old grits, looked the other way.
"Mess up what you can, boy," they'd say

with a wink, "*While* you can, boy."
Not that there was anything illegal, exactly;
the peace was always kept.

On the main road out of town,
though, battle-lines were clearly drawn.
Every night, headlights forced starlight

to bubble up from the tar; while in the daytime,
sunshine grew out of crossed mica-slivers.
Violence lulled me.

I had my big wreck and come-uppance that way.
Oh, how I'd wanted to take her out.
It was a scalding Fourth, and we got drunk.

My heart was an oiled engine, racing.
For once, the charm on the rear-view failed.
My eyes were bewildered:

All I remember is the tail-lights
of her father's pickup
before I blew him clear the hell out of sight.

The good old days are over,
and peace is history;
and that's why I left home

and that's why I have no home.

# At Forrest Park

You pricked your way through Tennessee:
A thorn in the Union side, you spurred
     your way back to Memphis,
and rode your horses right into the lobby
     of the best hotel in town,
astonishing the Yankee soldiers occupying its plush
     chairs with their behinds, and their time
with the local paper Grant hijacked.
     The commotion you caused
on the cobblestone boulevards,
     especially as your saber rent
the blue Southern sky, drew the cheers
     of the town's finest citizens.
Later, they threw you a parade. A brass band
     played "Dixie" to celebrate
the accelerated music of your heartbeat and gall.
     Crowds rebel-yelled, roustabouts pick-pocketed,
and horses snorted and neighed in the dust.
     But the day,
the glory, have left precious little
     behind, battlefield blood
has long since annealed into salty clay
     till nothing but the bone
of free land remains; and all the agony,
     the honor and the dishonor,
are fodder now for videos and books.
     Erected by your countrymen,
your Parisian-forged effigy
     faces the subdued
red brick of an abandoned Sealtest factory, and your horse
     treads marble, not crimsoned sod.
Your face is gilded with consternation,
     as if you were asking

directions in your own hometown.
 Time and traffic have tattooed
the border of your saddle. All metal and composure
 in this poorly kept park,
where can you ride now?
 The men and women who cut
through to reach Union Avenue
 are the descendants of those whose enslavement
 you defended, and the flag you defied furls
 and unfurls like a contented cat's tail
over the tiny square of land ceded to you.
 Only the squirrels here,
and occasionally the weather, are still
 grey; there's a ragtag line
of mismatched lampposts, and the hedges are clipped
 spare, and look starved.
A skyline rises at your elbow:
 Memphis
barely acknowledges you now.
 Lee's
Family Restaurant, with its "home-cooked soul-food,"
 the Pyramid,
glittering in white-washed promise,
 intrude, while the river,
under the bluff a mile off,
 rushes away to New Orleans.
I, too, intrude;
 and if I can't quite
make my peace with you, General,
 I can bring you this news:
that all around us, Sir,
 the nation still suffers
its successes and defeats,
 that we remain at war among ourselves.
Slavery has ended, but

             the gangstas don't care
about old battles fought here—
             their latest ambitions and bloodlusts
will rename these streets.
             Maybe they, like you, will teach history a lesson,
though it's hard to read one now
             in the glazed-over eyes of the naked windows
of washed-up clothing stores
             and run-down shoe shops
on the failed Mid-America Mall.
             Facades of fallen buildings look like grit
teeth on unlovingly reconstructed Beale St.,
             where waitresses and guides talk proudly
of brand-new cafes and museums of Southern culture.
             Only the eponymous Mr. Schwab in his general store
keeps the void at bay,
             retailing merchandise ancient
as his stories. It amounts to this:
             War, when it comes,
is fast and furious, forgetfulness
             slow but sure;
as the bumper sticker says,
             "Shit happens."
You are stuck here forever,
             General Forrest,
without so much as a ghost to talk to.
             Memphis
is sick and tired of the past.
             Day after day,
her city limits reach farther
             and farther away.

# To the Angels

On still-haunted Main Street
tourist trolleys rattle the bones

of unreconstructed storefronts;
I feel the cobblestones shudder as

I watch a torn wisp of cotton
blow past from the Cotton

Exchange, and look at my watch
though I already know the time.

Heat rises, my hand falls,
there is always proof of earth:

one black cloud follows one white as
light takes on the endless responsibility of shape;

at the river's rough lip, birds circle, and bees hive,
a concatenation of the beautifully unworkable;

just so, an hour slides, history gives way:
first the light, then the night, then the quietly abjuring angels.

# Union

*With these songs, sole comfort*
—Sterling A. Brown

The bridge is there
for crossing or not

On the other side
lies the fabled West

I come with a guitar
slung over my shoulder

The song I sing
comes from the heart of wood

The notes I play
are lost, lost, and lost

      *

On Union Avenue
a long

siren yawns

Lights change slow and grand
from here to the river

The river slouches on
from here to the Delta

Perhaps there is no
siren or man here

Just river

*

Tonight I saw
the moon enter the river

It slid past the bluff
through the sunken dogwood

left a sheen
on the levee

while the black-hearted river
froze into whitecaps

and the Mississippi turned
all into ice:

Mississippi ice

*

No birds luffed
upward here

The Arkansaw wind
is dry and starved

It rasps the heft
off the hogs' bones

It brings yellow fever

The Arkansaw wind
is a skilled hand

*

The river is where
time is illegible

The river rushes past
without rushing

past Memphis
where a drowned flag rises

Where America folds in
on itself and against itself

Where the United States ends
and begins

The Mississippi is
a long American wound

      *

When geese fly out
to Mud Island why do they stop?

Rock by rock
the riverway leads noplace

leads noplace
but the brownskin river

the river the birds
recognize

A body of water
Mirror of dry souls

Who knows Memphis?

Memphis was born
from abolished ruins

Memphis forgot
that Memphis is guilt

Step by step
its folks wade down

in groaning steps
till they damn near drown

in robes of thick mud

Dismantled city
Throne of noplace

                *

Memphis is
two syllables

I say each one
by the statue over the bones

Of General Forrest

near the medical school
where black doctors train

who go back
to parts of town

where anger
never cedes

from old
cracked lips

lisping
"Memphis"

      *

A tall reedy man
fishes by the bridge

I find him there
singing

Under the bridge
farther along

I hear more
than the water

I hear more
than his blues

I hear something
scratching

A swarm of rats
Our rats

Confederates

      *

The terms
of river warfare

are obscure

Tom Lee Park
when blanked out

with snow
(it does snow)

shows no sign
of catastrophe

of blues
or yellow fever

of the humid months
of blood and dust

of war lost

of the South's ghost
disgraced

but the monuments
engraved and broken

leave their marks

and contain understanding
forever:

The South has gone down
and it will not come up

    *

Ma Rainey
is gone

who would show
you through here

this stone, that stone
like fallen Bibles

If there were

a book of Memphis
it would be a book

of the dead
It would have no words

only blues
blues like a Gulf

storm whipping up
the Mississippi

shaking the pernicious
magnolia

slapping the dogwood
leaves till they weep

strumming the plumed
factory smoke

then blowing a last
gasp

of cotton
down Front Street

by the Cotton
Exchange

and hearing
all these blues

the afternoon
would grow dark

then the afternoon
would grow light

then the sun would
set as if

nothing ever happened

no note added
or taken away

And you would hear
that this water-eyed blues

is not a bitter blues

I try to hum
by Ma Rainey's grave

a few broken bars

\*

The rain
throws down lead

bullets of rain
over a beaten city

with no horizon

Beneath the river we see
is the river we do not see

Drowned water

Cruel rain
Cruel river:

*Better be movin'*
*Better be travelin' on*
*Mississippi get you*
*If you stay*

In the hearing
of our ancestors:

*You better move some*
*Better not get rooted*
*Muddy water fool you*
*If you stay*

The river so close
The past so close

　　　*

Now the river swells
its wet lungs

and threatens
to rise again

In truth all
its currents flow

like knuckled roots
into one lonesome earth

# Arch

A god, a road, a woman.
Bows of promise, given.
The Mississippi River Bridge in the sun.

Triumphal heat in the sun's reflection.
Among unmortared bricks, a keystone.
A god, a road, a woman.

A principal, and a principle: a tradition.
The broad bend of Heaven.
The Mississippi River Bridge in the sun.

Rome's raging empire; a vault in
Air; the cope of a calyx, a fortification.
A god, a road, a woman.

Hunter with quiver, the moon far risen,
His raised brow, hidden.
The Mississippi River Bridge in the sun.

A cat's unexpected turn.
The grace of fingers, and spoon.
A god, a road, a woman.
The Mississippi River Bridge in the sun.

# Notes

"Self-portrait in the I-Zone™": I-Zone is a registered trademark of the Polaroid Corporation.

The opening lines of "Union" are very loosely adapted from Mario Benedetti's poem in Spanish, "El Puente."

The italicized stanzas in the penultimate section of the poem are adapted from Sterling A. Brown's poem, "Riverbank Blues."